Handy North Dakota Handbook

I0450173

Gary L. Morris

©2015 Gary L. Morris

ISBN-13: 978-1507758731

ISBN-10: 1507758731

Table of Contents

Notes

Genealogical Research in North Dakota

There are many genealogical records and resources available for tracing your family history in North Dakota. Because there are so many records held at many different locations, tracking down the records for your ancestor can be an ominous task. Don't worry though, we know just where they are, and we'll show you which records you'll need, while helping you to understand:

1. What they are
2. Where to find them
3. How to use them

These records can be found both online and off, so we'll introduce you to online websites, indexes and databases, as well as brick-and-mortar repositories and other institutions that will help with your research in North Dakota. So that you will have a more comprehensive understanding of these records, we have provided a brief history of the "Rough Rider State" to illustrate what type of records may have been generated during specific time periods. That information will assist you in pinpointing times and locations on which to focus the search for your North Dakota ancestors and their records.

A Brief History of North Dakota

The Sioux and the Ojibwa were the main Native American tribes inhabiting the area we now know as North Dakota when the first Europeans arrived in 1738. The French fur trader Pierre Gaultier de Varennes was the first to enter the region, and fur trading spread rapidly through the Missouri and red River valleys. After the Lewis and Clark expedition explored the Missouri from 1804–1806, the American Fur Company was established and specialized in providing Buffalo hides to consumers.

Scottish settlers flocked to the area around Pembina, while the trading of buffalo hides continued. The Scottish settlers introduced farming to the region, and much of the labor came from métis, who were of missed Native American and European origin. The area remained relatively trouble free until the influx of white settlers during and after the Civil war. The Sioux put up resistance, but the superior power and resources of the white settlers resulted in them signing treaties which confined them to reservations.

The arrival of the Northern Pacific Railroad at Fargo in 1872 and its extension to the Missouri the year after led to the rise of homesteading on giant "bonanza farms," and settlers flocked to the area, especially from Canada. The "boom" was short lived however, and drought combined with depressed farm prices led to many of the initial Canadian and American settlers abandoning the region. Germans, Norwegians, and other Europeans replaced the Americans and Canadians who had left, and when North Dakota entered the Union in 1889, North Dakota had one of the highest populations of foreign-born residents.

Important Dates in North Dakota History

1803 – United States receives North Dakota as part of the Louisiana Purchase

1818 – Northeastern part of the region ceded from Great Britain to the United States

1834 – Part of Michigan Territory

1836 – Part of Wisconsin Territory

1838 – Part of Iowa Territory

1849 – Part of Minnesota Territory

1854 – Part of Nebraska Territory

1861 – Reorganized as Dakota Territory

1889 – Territory of Dakota divided into North and South Dakota

Famous Battles Fought in North Dakota

There were no Revolutionary War or Civil War battles fought in North Dakota, but the area was directly affected by a Sioux Uprising in 1862, of which the most influential battle was the **Battle of Big Mound**.

These battle accounts that exist can be very effective in uncovering the military records of your ancestor. They can tell you what regiments fought in which battles, and often include the names and ranks of many officers and enlisted men.

For information on other battles fought during the Sioux Uprising you can visit the **North Dakota Indian Battles** website.

Battle of Big Mound:
http://www.nps.gov/hps/abpp/battles/nd001.htm

North Dakota Indian Battles: http://indianbattles.weebly.com/

Common North Dakota Genealogical Issues and Resources to Overcome Them

Boundary Changes: Boundary changes are a common obstacle when researching North Dakota ancestors. You could be searching for an ancestor's record in one county when in fact it is stored in a different one due to historical county boundary changes.

The **Atlas of Historical County Boundaries** can help you to overcome that problem. It provides a chronological listing of every boundary change that has occurred in the history of North Dakota.

Atlas of Historical County Boundaries:
http://publications.newberry.org/ahcbp/documents/ND_Consolidated _Chronology.htm#Consolidated_Chronology

Name Changes: Surname changes, variations, and misspellings can complicate genealogical research. It is important to check all spelling variations. Soundex, a program that indexes names by sound, is a useful first step, but you can't rely on it completely as some name variations result in different Soundex codes. The surnames could be different, but the first name may be different too. You can also find records filed under initials, middle names, and nicknames as well, so you will need to **get creative with surname variations** and spellings in order to cover all the possibilities. For help with surname variations read our instructional article on **How to Use Soundex**.

get creative with surname variations:
http://obituarieshelp.org/blog/?p=634

How to Use Soundex: http://obituarieshelp.org/blog/?p=505

North Dakota Genealogical Organizations and Archives

Genealogical resources include not only records, but the organizations that house them, or can direct you to them. These institutions include: *Archives, Libraries, Genealogical Societies, Family History Centers, Universities, Churches, and Museums.*

Following are links to their websites, their physical addresses, and a summary of the records you can find there.

Archives and Libraries

State Historical Society of North Dakota (State Archives) – federal census from 1850, Native American census schedules, territorial census, district court records, 1861-1889, military records, historical newspapers, oral histories, naturalization index, death index, and more

612 East Boulevard Ave.
Bismarck, North Dakota 58505
Tel: (701) 328-2666
Fax: (701) 328-3710
Email: histsoc@nd.gov

State Historical Society of North Dakota (State Archives):
http://history.nd.gov/archives/genealogy.html

National Archives Rocky Mountain Region (Denver) - Federal population censuses for all States, 1790-1930, Revolutionary War records, Pension and bounty land warrant applications, Ship's passenger lists, Native American censuses

National Archives at Denver
17101 Huron Street
Broomfield, CO 80023
Telephone: 303-604-4740
Fax: 303-407-5707

National Archives Rocky Mountain Region:
http://www.archives.gov/denver/public/genealogy.html

Chester Fritz Library – family histories, county marriage licenses, inquest reports, dating from 1882-1989, land records dating from 1883

University of North Dakota
Grand Forks, ND 58202-9000
Tel: 701-777-4625

Chester Fritz Library: http://library.und.edu/special-collections/genealogy.php

North Dakota Genealogical and Historical Societies

Genealogical and historical societies have access to extensive catalogues of genealogical data. They are also able to offer expert guidance for genealogical researchers. Many members are professional genealogists who are most willing to share their expertise in finding ancestors.

Bismarck-Mandan Historical and Genealogical Society – variety of genealogical resources and research assistance including; cemetery records, school records, funeral home records, newspapers, church records, marriage records, and census records

PO Box 485
Bismarck, ND 58502-0485
Email: info@bmhgs.com

Bismarck-Mandan Historical and Genealogical Society:
http://www.bmhgs.com/

Germans from Russia Heritage Society – family histories, cemetery records, chirch histories, surname database, passenger lists, church histories

1125 West Turnpike Avenue
Bismarck, North Dakota 58501
Telephone: (701) 223-6167
Fax: (701) 223-4421

Germans from Russia Heritage Society: http://www.grhs.org/

Red River Valley Genealogical Society – Pioneers lists, Tombstone transcriptions, Funeral Homes index, Genealogy books (especially many publications on Norwegian ancestry).

PO Box 9284
Fargo, ND 58106

112 N. University Dr.
Suite L-116
Fargo ND 58106-9284

Red River Valley Genealogical Society:
http://www.redrivergenealogy.com/index.htm

North Dakota Mailing Lists

Mailing lists are internet based facilities that use email to distribute a single message to all who subscribe to it. When information on a particular surname, new records, or any other important genealogy information related to the mailing list topic becomes available, the subscribers are alerted to it. Joining a mailing list is an excellent way to stay up to date on North Dakota genealogy research topics. Rootsweb have an extensive listing of **North Dakota Mailing Lists** on a variety of topics.

North Dakota Mailing Lists:
http://lists.rootsweb.ancestry.com/index/usa/ND/misc.html

North Dakota Message Boards

A message board is another internet based facility where people can post questions about a specific genealogy topic and have it answered by other genealogists. If you have questions about a surname, record type, or research topic, you can post your question and other researchers and genealogists will help you with the answer. Be sure to check back regularly, as the answers are not emailed to you. The North Dakota message boards at **Rootsweb** are completely free to use.

Rootsweb:
http://boards.rootsweb.com/localities.northam.usa.states/mb.ashx

North Dakota Newspapers and Periodicals

Many genealogy periodicals and historical newspapers contain reprinted copies of family genealogies, transcripts of family Bible records, information about local records and archives, census indexes, church records, queries, land records, obituaries, court records, cemetery records, and wills. The following sites have historical North Dakota newspapers and periodicals that you can search online or on-site.

State Historical Society of North Dakota (State Archives) – large collection of newspapers covering every county in North Dakota

612 East Boulevard Ave.
Bismarck, North Dakota 58505
Tel: (701) 328-2666
Fax: (701) 328-3710
Email: histsoc@nd.gov

State Historical Society of North Dakota (State Archives):
http://history.nd.gov/archives/newsndpapers.html

North Dakota State University Libraries - North Dakota newspaper collection, 1860s-2000s

P.O. Box 5599
Fargo, ND 58105-5599
Phone: (701) 231-8914

North Dakota State University Libraries:
http://library.ndsu.edu/repository/handle/10365/22597

GenealogyBank.com – free searchable database of North Dakota newspaper archives, 1979-1923

GenealogyBank.com:
http://www.genealogybank.com/gbnk/newspapers/explore/USA/Nort h_Dakota/

The Online Books Page – links to historical North Dakota books and periodicals available for viewing online

The Online Books Page: http://onlinebooks.library.upenn.edu

Library of Congress Digital Newspaper Directory – free searchable database of historical U.S. newspapers dating from 1690-present

Library of Congress Digital Newspaper Directory: http://chroniclingamerica.loc.gov/search/titles/

NewspaperArchive.com – largest online database of historical newspapers in the world.

NewspaperArchive.com: http://newspaperarchive.com/

Historical North Dakota Maps and Gazetteers

Maps are an integral part of genealogical research. They help us to locate landmarks, towns, cities, parishes, states, provinces, waterways and roads and streets. They also help us to determine when and where boundary changes might have taken place, and give us a visualization of the area we're researching in.

For locating place names, a gazetteer is the best possible resource for any genealogist. Gazetteers are also sometimes called "place name dictionaries", and can help you to locate the area in which you need to conduct research. Below are links to the maps and gazetteers for research in North Dakota.

Peabody GNIS Service – North Dakota:
http://peabody.research.yale.edu/cgi-bin/Query.GNIS?ST=North%20Dakota&SU=1

Color Landform Atlas – North Dakota:
http://fermi.jhuapl.edu/states/nd_0.html

1985 U.S. Atlas: http://www.livgenmi.com/1895/ND/

North Dakota Hometown Locator:
http://northdakota.hometownlocator.com/

North Dakota City Directories

.

City directories are similar to telephone directories in that they list the residents of a particular area. The difference though is what is important to genealogists, and that is they pre-date telephone directories. You can find an ancestor's information such as their street address, place of employment, occupation, or the name of their spouse. A one-stop-shop for finding city directories in North Dakota is the **North Dakota Online Historical Directories** which contains a listing of every available online historical directory related to North Dakota.

North Dakota Online Historical Directories:
https://sites.google.com/site/onlinedirectorysite/Home/usa/nd

Additionally the **Grand Forks Public Library** has an city directories from 1882-1977

2110 Library Circle
Grand Forks, ND, United States
Tel: 701-772-8116

422 4th Street Northwest
East Grand Forks, MN, United States
Tel: 218-773-9121

Grand Forks Public Library:
http://www.gflibrary.com/index.aspx?nid=243

North Dakota Genealogical Records

Birth, Death, Marriage and Divorce Records – Also known as vital records, birth, death, and marriage certificates are the most basic, yet most important records attached to your ancestor. The reason for their importance is that they not only place your ancestor in a specific place at a definite time, but potentially connect the individual to other relatives. Below is a list of repositories and websites where you can find North Dakota vital records.

Marriage and divorce records are held by **North Dakota Clerks of the County Court** in the county where the event occurred.

North Dakota Clerks of the County Court:
http://ndhealth.gov/vital/marriage.htm

North Dakota Division of Vital Records – births, deaths, fetal deaths 1883-present

North Dakota Division of Vital Records: http://ndhealth.gov/vital/

State Historical Society of North Dakota (State Archives) – pre-1925 marriage records from the following counties: Barnes, Emmons, McHenry, Morton, Steele, Walsh, and Ward

612 East Boulevard Ave.
Bismarck, North Dakota 58505
Tel: (701) 328-2666
Fax: (701) 328-3710
Email: histsoc@nd.gov

State Historical Society of North Dakota (State Archives):
http://history.nd.gov/archives/newsndpapers.html

Chester Fritz Library – Searchable index of over 9,700 county marriage certificates, dating from November 1875 to June 30, 1925

University of North Dakota
Grand Forks, ND 58202-9000
Tel: 701-777-4625

Chester Fritz Library: http://library.und.edu/special-collections/genealogy.php

Census Reports

Census records are among the most important genealogical documents for placing your ancestor in a particular place at a specific time. Like BDM records, they can also lead you to other ancestors, particularly those who were living under the authority of the head of household.

Federal census records for North Dakota exist from 1850–1930 and can be found at:

State Historical Society of North Dakota (State Archives) – federal census from 1850, Native American census schedules, territorial census
612 East Boulevard Ave.
Bismarck, North Dakota 58505
Tel: (701) 328-2666
Fax: (701) 328-3710
Email: histsoc@nd.gov

State Historical Society of North Dakota (State Archives):
http://history.nd.gov/archives/genealogy.html

National Archives Rocky Mountain Region (Denver) - Federal population censuses for all States, 1790-1930, Native American censuses

National Archives at Denver
17101 Huron Street
Broomfield, CO 80023
Telephone: 303-604-4740
Fax: 303-407-5707

National Archives Rocky Mountain Region :
http://www.archives.gov/denver/public/genealogy.html

National Archives – Federal census Schedules for all states, 1790-1940

8601 Adelphi Road
College Park, MD 20740-6001
Tel: 1-866-272-6272

National Archives: http://www.archives.gov/research/census/

The **Free Census Project** has transcribed many North Dakota indexes and new material is added daily

Free Census Project: http://usgwcensus.org/cenfiles/nd.htm

Access Genealogy – North Dakota county census records from 1880-1930

Access Genealogy: http://www.accessgenealogy.com/census/north-dakota-census-records.htm

African American Census Schedules Online – slave schedules, mortality schedules, slave-owners census

African American Census Schedules Online:
http://www.afrigeneas.com/aacensus/ga/

Native Americans in Census Records (US National Archives):
http://www.archives.gov/research/census/native-americans/

North Dakota Church Records

Church and synagogue records are a valuable resource, especially for baptisms, marriages, and burials that took place before 1900. You will need to at least have an idea of your ancestor's religious denomination, and in most cases you will have to visit a brick and mortar establishment to view them.

Most church records are kept by the individual church, although in some denominations, records are placed in a regional archive or maintained at the diocesan level. Local Historical Societies are sometimes the repository for the state's older church records. Below are links archives that maintain church records, as well as a few databases that can be viewed online.

The **Family History Library** contains many church records from a variety of denominations on microfilm.

Family History Library:
http://familysearch.org/learn/wiki/en/Family_History_Library

Central Repositories for Denominational Records

Church of Jesus Christ of Latter-day Saints (Mormons)

Early Mormon Church records for North Dakota can be found on film located at the LDS Family History Library in Salt Lake City and can be searched via the **Family History Library Catalog**

Family History Library Catalog:
https://familysearch.org/eng/Library/FHLC/frameset_fhlc.asp

Lutheran

Evangelical Lutheran Church in America
(ELCA Archives)
8765 W. Higgins Road
Chicago, IL 60631-4198
Phone: (800) 638-3522 or (773) 380-2700
Fax: (773) 380-1465
Email: archives@elca.org

Evangelical Lutheran Church in Americao:
http://www.elca.org/ELCA/Contact-Us.aspx

Many Lutheran Church records for Germans from Russia are at:

Institute for Regional Studies
North Dakota State University Libraries
P.O. Box 5599
Fargo, ND 58105-5599
Phone: (701) 231-8914
Fax: (701) 231-5632
Email: archives@www.lib.ndsu.nodak.edu

Institute for Regional Studies: http://library.ndsu.edu/repository/

Methodist

United Methodist Church
North Dakota Conference
Wesley United Methodist Church
1600 4th Ave North
Grand Forks, ND 58203
Phone: (701) 772-1869

North Dakota Conference: http://www.dakotasumc.org/

McGovern Library
Dakota Wesleyan University
Box 460
1200 West University Avenue
Mitchell, SD 57301-4398
Phone: (605) 995-2618
Fax: (605) 995-2893
Email: library@dwu.edu

McGovern Library: http://www.dwu.edu/library/

Presbyterian

Presbyterian Historical Society
United Presbyterian Church in the U.S.
425 Lombard Street
Philadelphia, PA 19147
Phone: (215) 627-1852
Fax: (215) 627-0509

Presbyterian Historical Society: http://history.pcusa.org/

Roman Catholic

Diocese of Bismarck
Chancery Office
Box 1575
420 Raymond Street
Bismarck, ND 58502-1575
Phone: (701) 223-1347
Fax: (701) 223-3693

Diocese of Bismarck link to: http://www.bismarckdiocese.com/

Diocese of Fargo
5201 Bishops Blvd., Suite A
Fargo, ND 58104-7605
Phone: (701) 356-7900

Diocese of Fargo: http://www.fargodiocese.org/

North Dakota Military Records

More than 40 million Americans have participated in some time of war service since America was colonized. The chance of finding your ancestor amongst those records is exceptionally high. Military records can even reveal individuals who never actually served, such as those who registered for the two World Wars but were never called to duty.

Below are a number of links to websites and archives that contain North Dakota military records.

State Historical Society of North Dakota (State Archives) – Service Records and Records of Veterans' Benefits

612 East Boulevard Ave.
Bismarck, North Dakota 58505
Tel: (701) 328-2666
Fax: (701) 328-3710
Email: histsoc@nd.gov

State Historical Society of North Dakota (State Archives): http://history.nd.gov/archives/genealogy.html

National Archives Rocky Mountain Region (Denver) - Revolutionary War records, Pension and bounty land warrant applications

National Archives at Denver
17101 Huron Street
Broomfield, CO 80023
Telephone: 303-604-4740
Fax: 303-407-5707

National Archives Rocky Mountain Region: http://www.archives.gov/denver/public/genealogy.html

US Department of Veterans Affairs Nationwide Gravesite Locator – includes information on veterans and their family members buried in veterans and military cemeteries having a government grave marker.

US Department of Veterans Affairs Nationwide Gravesite Locator: http://gravelocator.cem.va.gov/

You may also find your ancestor's military records in the following databases:

United States General Index to Pension Files, 1861-1934: https://familysearch.org/search/collection/1919699

United States Index to Service Records, War with Spain, 1898: https://familysearch.org/search/collection/1919583

United States Index to Indian Wars Pension Files, 1892-1926 – military pension records of soldiers who fought in the Indian Wars between 1817 and 1898

United States Index to Indian Wars Pension Files, 1892-1926: https://familysearch.org/search/collection/1979427

United States Registers of Enlistments in the U.S. Army, 1798-1914: https://familysearch.org/search/collection/1880762

United States Mexican War Pension Index, 1887-1926 - index to Mexican War pension files for service between 1846 and 1848

United States Mexican War Pension Index, 1887-1926: https://familysearch.org/search/collection/1979390

Civil War Soldiers Service Records - Service records for both Union and Confederate soldiers indexed by soldier's name, rank, and unit.

Civil War Soldier Service Records: http://go.fold3.com/civilwar_records/

North Dakota Cemetery Records

As convenient as it is to search cemetery records online, keep in mind that there are a few disadvantages over visiting a cemetery in person. They are:

1. Tombstone information is not always accurately transcribed
2. The arrangement of the graves in a cemetery can be crucial as family members are often buried next to each other or in the same grave. This arrangement is not always preserved in the alphabetical indexes that are found online.

With that information in mind, the following websites have databases that can be searched online for North Dakota Cemetery records.

North Dakota Tombstone Transcription Project - death and burial records

North Dakota Tombstone Transcription Project:
http://www.usgwtombstones.org/northdakota/ndakota.html

Red River Valley Genealogical Society – Tombstone transcriptions, Funeral Homes index

Mailing Address:
PO Box 9284
Fargo, ND 58106

Physical Location:
112 N. University Dr.
Suite L-116
Fargo ND 58106-9284

Red River Valley Genealogical Society:
http://www.redrivergenealogy.com/index.htm

African American Cemeteries Online – African American, slave, and Native American cemetery records

African American Cemeteries Online: http://africanamericancemeteries.com

Access Genealogy – database of North Dakota cemetery record transcriptions

Access Genealogy: http://www.accessgenealogy.com/cemetery/north-dakota-cemetery-records.htm

Find a Grave – over 100 million grave records can be searched on this site. Search can be conducted by name, location, or cemetery name.

Find a Grave: http://www.findagrave.com/

Interment.net - A free online database containing approximately 4 million cemetery records from around the world.

Interment.net: http://www.interment.net/

Billion Graves – as the name implies, you can search a billion records including headstone photos, transcriptions, cemetery records, and grave locations.

Billion Graves: http://billiongraves.com/pages/search/index.php#cemetery

North Dakota Obituaries

Obituaries can reveal a wealth about our ancestor and other relatives. You can search our **North Dakota Newspaper Obituaries Listings** from hundreds of North Dakota newspapers online for free.

North Dakota Newspaper Obituaries Listings: http://obituarieshelp.org/north_dakota_newspaper_obituaries.html

North Dakota Wills and Probate Records

The documents found in a probate packet may include a complete inventory of a person's estate, newspaper entries, witness testimony, a copy of a will, list of debtors and creditors, names of executors or trustees, names of heirs. They can not only tell you about the ancestor you're currently researching, but lead to other ancestors.

North Dakota probate records are held by **North Dakota Clerks of the County Court** in the county where the event occurred.

North Dakota Clerks of the County Court:
http://www.ndcourts.gov/court/counties/dc_clerk/members.htm

North Dakota Immigration and Naturalization Records

The naturalization process generated many types of records, including petitions, declarations of intention, and oaths of allegiance. These records can provide family historians with information such as a person's birth date and place of birth, immigration year, marital status, spouse information, occupation, witnesses' names and addresses, and more.

State Historical Society of North Dakota (State Archives) – naturalization index covering the period up to 1955

612 East Boulevard Ave.
Bismarck, North Dakota 58505
Tel: (701) 328-2666
Fax: (701) 328-3710
Email: histsoc@nd.gov

State Historical Society of North Dakota (State Archives) :
http://history.nd.gov/archives/genealogy.html

National Archives Rocky Mountain Region (Denver) - Atlantic ports Indexes 1820-1952, Passenger Lists 1820-1948, Baltimore, MD Index 1820-1952, Passenger Lists 1820-1909, Boston, MA, Index 1848-1891, 1902-1906, Passenger Lists 1820-1943, Galveston, TX Index 1896-1951, Passenger Lists 1896-1951, Gulf ports Indexes 1890-1924, New Orleans, LA, Index 1853-1899, Passenger Lists 1820-1902, New York, NY, Index 1820-1848, 1897-1943, Passenger Lists 1820-1957, Philadelphia, PA, Index 1800-1948, Passenger Lists 1800-1945, St. Albans, VT (Canadian entries), Indexes 1894-1952, Passenger Lists 1929-1949

National Archives at Denver
17101 Huron Street
Broomfield, CO 80023
Telephone: 303-604-4740
Fax: 303-407-5707

National Archives Rocky Mountain Region:
http://www.archives.gov/denver/public/genealogy.html

North Dakota Native American Records

State Historical Society of North Dakota (State Archives) –Native American census schedules, territorial census

612 East Boulevard Ave.
Bismarck, North Dakota 58505
Tel: (701) 328-2666
Fax: (701) 328-3710
Email: histsoc@nd.gov

State Historical Society of North Dakota (State Archives):
http://history.nd.gov/archives/genealogy.html

National Archives Rocky Mountain Region (Denver) - Native American censuses

National Archives at Denver
17101 Huron Street
Broomfield, CO 80023
Telephone: 303-604-4740
Fax: 303-407-5707

National Archives Rocky Mountain Region:
http://www.archives.gov/denver/public/genealogy.html

Access Genealogy – North Dakota Native American census records, tribal histories, and much more

Access Genealogy: http://www.accessgenealogy.com/native/north-dakota-indian-tribes.htm

U.S. National Archives - information on American Indians who maintained their ties to Federally-recognized Tribes (1830-1970).

U.S. National Archives: http://www.archives.gov/research/native-americans/

Records of the Bureau of Indian Affairs (BIA)

Records of the Bureau of Indian Affairs (BIA):
http://www.archives.gov/research/guide-fed-records/groups/075.html

American Indians Records Repository - records dating from the 1700s including trust, education and other historic Indian Affairs records

American Indian Records Repository
Meritex Enterprises
17501 West 98th Street
Lenexa, KS 66219
Phone: 913-888-0601

American Indians Records Repository:
http://www.doi.gov/ost/records_mgmt/american-indian-records-repository.cfm

Missing Matriarchs – Resources for Researching Female North Dakota Ancestors

Looking for female ancestors requires an adjustment of how we view traditional records sources. A woman's identity was often under that of her husband, and often individual records for them can be difficult to locate. The following resources are effective in locating female ancestors in North Dakota where traditional records may not reveal them.

<u>Bibliographies</u>

1. *The Quiet Conquest: A History of the Life and Times of the First Settlers of Central North Dakota,* Barbara Levorsen (The Hawley Herald, 1974)
2. *Prairie Mosaic: An Ethnic Atlas of Rural North Dakota,* William C. Sherman (North Dakota Institute for Regional Studies, 1983)
3. *Daughters of Dacotah,* Stella Marie Stutenroth (Eduction Supply Co., n.d)

Selected Resources for North Dakota Women's History

Barns County Historical Museum
PO Box 188
Valley City, ND 58072

Chester Fritz Library
University of North Dakota
Grand Forks, ND 58202

North Dakota Institute for Regional Studies
North Dakota State University Library
PO Boxx 5599
Fargo, ND 58105-5599

Common North Dakota Surnames

The following surnames are among the most common in North Dakota and are also being currently researched by other genealogists. If you find your surname here, there is a chance that some research has already been performed on your ancestor.

Baldwin, Barkema, Bissell, Bolles, Bruster, Buckingham, Buell, Cambridge, Cawley, Chaffee, Chapman, Chas, Child, Clifton, Colburn, Cole, Colpitts, Cooper, Corbin, Davis, DeCamp, Delano, Dendy, Dent, Dicker, Dobson, Douglas, Duckworth, Duerrbaum, Eastman, Elizabeth, Ellsworth, Engel, Erickson, Fakler, Filly, Gamer, Garrard, Geringer, Geschwind, Grant, Gumbert, Hanson, Harris, Harrison, Herwig, Honore, Hull, Huntington, Hyland, Jenkins, John, Johnson, Jones, Kangas, Kelly, Kilponen, Knights, Komulainen, Kyllonen, Leachland, Levett, Ligon, Liimatta, Lindquist, Lyders, Lyman, Lyon, Lyons, Markert, Mary, Medary, Middlebrook, Minor, Morris, Okland, Paananen, Pagan, Palmer, Paso, Peck, Piirainen, Pinney, Porter, Prairie, Priscilla, Proudfit, Pulkkinen, Puryear, Rademacher, Rathbone, Rebecca, Richardson, Rodgerson, Rogers, Ruth, Sandberg, Sande, Schonfeld, Schroeder, Seely, Simpson, Sorbeo, Stoughton, Tervonen, Terway, Terwei, Todd, Tormanen, Turner, Veeder, Viets, Wagoner, Waits, Ward, Whipple, Wilkins, Will, Witter, Wolcott

About the Author

Gary L. Morris worked from 2009 to 2014 as a professional researcher for a major player in the genealogy field. After tracing his family lineage back to 1683, he found that genealogy could be an expensive undertaking. As such, has decided to publish these helpful guides to share the valuable free information he has discovered during his career to help others trace their family lineages as inexpensively as possible. An avid genealogist himself, he hopes you will find this guide factual, thorough, helpful, and most of all, effective in helping you to find your family members.

Notes

Notes

www.ingramcontent.com/pod-product-compliance
Lightning Source LLC
Chambersburg PA
CBHW061935280526
45787CB00004B/1608